AF348897

Made in the USA
Monee, IL
07 July 2026

56551524R00069